BEHIND
THE
SCENES

A Ghostly Tale

BEHIND THE SCENES

A Ghostly Tale

Written by Meredith Costain

RANDOM HOUSE AUSTRALIA

A Random House book
Published by Random House Australia Pty Ltd
Level 3, 100 Pacific Highway, North Sydney NSW 2060
www.randomhouse.com.au

First published by Random House Australia in 2012

Addresses for companies within the Random House Group can be found at
www.randomhouse.com.au/offices.

National Library of Australia
Cataloguing-in-Publication Entry

Author: Irwin, Bindi, 1998–
Title: Bindi Behind the Scenes: A Ghostly Tale /
Bindi Irwin, Meredith Costain
ISBN: 978 1 86471 844 7 (pbk)
Series: Irwin, Bindi, 1998– Bindi behind the scenes; 6.
Target audience: For primary school age
Other authors/contributors: Costain, Meredith
Dewey number: A823.4

Cover photograph © Australia Zoo
Cover and internal design by Christabella Designs
Typeset by Midland Typesetters, Australia
Printed in Australia by Griffin Press, an accredited ISO AS/NZS
14001:2004 Environmental Management System printer

Random House Australia uses papers that are natural, renewable and
recyclable products and made from wood grown in sustainable forests.
The logging and manufacturing processes are expected to conform to the
environmental regulations of the country of origin.

Dear Diary,

I always thought I knew pretty much everything
there was to know about animals. Living in a place
like Australia Zoo and having a family like mine, it's
hard not to!

Feeding habits, lifespans, sizes and shapes,
conservation statuses – my friends call me a
walking, talking animal encyclopaedia. Until I went
to stay with old friends of my dad's up in the Top
End. While I was there, I discovered a new species
of animal that's not only rare, it's incredibly clever
and cute!

But sadly, that's not the only thing I discovered.
Something is threatening our northern beaches and
beautiful marine creatures – something that needs
to be stopped. But how? This was the big question

facing my friends who live in the remote coastal town I was visiting.

Fortunately, we found a way to help put things back on track. There's still a lot of work to do, but at least we know we're heading in the right direction – which brings me to life lesson number six:

kids can make a difference!

Let me tell you how ...

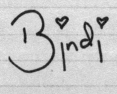

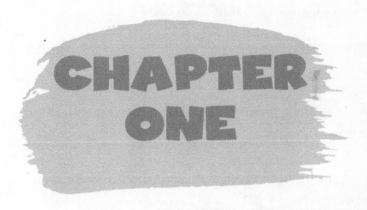

CHAPTER ONE

'YOU WANT ME TO DO WHAT?!'

Cushla McBride stared at Bindi, her eyes wide with alarm.

'Sit on the croc's head,' Bindi repeated, amused by her new friend's reaction. 'Don't worry, he won't bite. At least, he won't once we get the rope around his jaws,' she teased.

Cushla shuddered. 'How can you be sure?'

'Because I've been jumping crocs all my life,' Bindi replied. 'Well, ever since I was eight years old, anyway. Haven't I, Robert?'

Her brother nodded solemnly. 'Don't worry, Cush. B's an ace at it.'

Bindi grinned, then pointed to the croc team standing nearby with ropes at the ready. 'Besides, the guys here will help keep the big bloke under control. Right, Stretch?'

A tall, lanky guy in a khaki uniform flourished his arm in a regal way, then bowed. 'Your wish is our command, B,' he said, making the rest of his team laugh.

Cushla bit her lip. 'M–maybe I'll just sit this one out,' she suggested, her voice trembling, 'and watch the experts in action.'

Bindi stared at her. 'Are you kidding? You've come halfway around the world for this experience. There's no point backing out now.'

Cushla's adventure had begun six months before when her family attended the annual Steve Irwin Day Gala Dinner in Brisbane. They'd travelled all the way from Ireland to visit relatives, and as soon as Cushla found out about the dinner, she'd persuaded her parents to go. She was mad keen about animals, and had been a Wildlife Warrior ever since she'd seen a TV documentary Bindi had filmed about orphaned baby orangutans.

The dinner featured an auction with wonderful prizes – including a chance to go croc-jumping in Far North Queensland with the Irwins. Cushla had been over the moon when she'd discovered her family held the winning bid. And now here they were, back in Australia, involved in the biggest adventure of their lives.

It had taken two long plane trips from Brisbane to get to the closest airport, then another 90 kilometres in a Range Rover along a bumpy dirt road, dodging muddy potholes the size of wild boar. Now she was standing on a riverbank in the middle of the Steve Irwin Wildlife Reserve, staring into the angry eyes of a five metre-long saltwater crocodile. She'd never been so scared!

'He's a big one, isn't he?' Stretch laughed as the giant croc thrashed about inside the trap. 'You'll have to think of a good name for him.'

Part of the prize for winning the auction was naming rights for one of the crocodiles in the Australia Zoo research project.

'I'm thinking Crusher,' Cushla said. 'Or . . . Monster.'

Robert smiled at her. 'He's not a monster; he's a living dinosaur. And he's beautiful. Look at his teeth.'

'That's what I'm trying *not* to do,' Cushla admitted. On the way to the reserve, Bindi and Robert had been entertaining her family with facts about salties. Stuff like how they had 68 razor-sharp teeth that could bite through flesh as though it were hot butter. Or how they will eat almost anything they can overpower, including animals even bigger than themselves, such as water buffalo. Or how they were considered to be dangerous if you intruded on their territory, which, she reminded herself, they were doing right now! She took another step back.

Stretch grabbed a length of rope from Josh, another member of the croc team. 'Okay, you little beauty,' he said, walking towards a large metal cage floating in a shallow part of the river.

The cage was covered with leafy branches to make it look less like a trap and more like the sort of hidey-hole a croc might enjoy visiting. The croc team had baited the trap with the carcass of a feral pig to lure the croc in, and it had worked perfectly. As soon as the croc grabbed the meat, the front gate of the trap had slammed shut.

Stretch peered into the cage. 'For now, let's just call you Super Croc, okay?'

Super Croc hissed in reply.

Carefully dropping a snout rope over the giant's top jaw, Stretch pulled it taut just behind its front teeth. Once the rope was secure, he opened the gate. Then, together with a few other members of the croc team, he began to haul Super Croc out of the trap and up the riverbank.

'Watch out!' Bindi's mum, Terri, called as the angry croc looked like it was about to death roll.

Cushla's father made a move to join the team, but her mother held him back. 'I think you'd better be leaving it to the experts, Martin,' she advised him.

Bindi nodded. 'She's right. If the croc moves into a death roll, you might get swept off your feet.' She turned to Cushla, grinning. 'Once this beautiful big boy has his jaws secured, you'll have your chance to get involved. There's nothing more incredible than getting up close to one of these modern-day dinosaurs!'

Cushla nodded. Her friends would definitely be amazed. She hoped someone was going to be taking lots of photos, or no one would believe her.

'Watch out!' Stretch suddenly called. 'He's rolling!'

Cushla watched from a safe distance, her heart in her mouth, as the massive crocodile twisted over and over, trying to break free from the rope around its top jaw.

'Why do you call that a death roll?' she asked Bindi. 'It looks to me like he wants to live.'

'It's what they do when they're trying to kill their prey,' Bindi explained. 'They clamp them with their jaws then roll over and over in the water, pulling the animal with them until it drowns. And if the animal is really big, they can even use the death roll to break it down into smaller pieces for eating.'

'Oh,' Cushla said, her face white. 'That's maybe too much information.'

'It's perfectly natural,' Bindi assured her. 'That's how crocs hunt. They can't just go to the supermarket for their food, like we do.'

'I guess,' Cushla said.

'He's just acting on instinct at the moment. Every time the guys pull on the rope, the croc reacts by death rolling, trying to escape. And it's actually a good thing for us that he's rolling around and around like that because he'll bind up his own jaws with the rope. This will make it safer for us when we jump the croc.'

'Thanks for reminding me,' Cushla said, wrinkling her nose.

'Are you ready, Bindi?' Stretch called. 'Just give us a sec till we get him up into the shade, then he's all yours.'

Bindi and Cushla watched as the wildlife team

hauled the giant croc across the flat and towards the trees, away from the punishing rays of the tropical Top End sun.

Bindi grabbed Cushla's hand. 'Come on, let's go. Remember, you're my backup. No matter what happens – however much he rears and thrashes – you have to hang in there.'

'Me?' stammered Cushla. '*I'm* your backup?'

Bindi grinned. 'Well, you and the rest of the team.' She waved at Stretch. 'Now?'

'Now.'

CHAPTER TWO

JUST LIKE BINDI HAD WATCHED her father do so many times before, she and six of the wildlife team jumped onto the croc, right down to his tail. It was like a giant game of 'stacks on'.

Seeing Cushla hesitate, Terri gently took her by the arm. 'Come on, Cush, we'll find a nice safe spot right in the middle here.'

Cushla took a deep breath, then joined the team pinning the giant saurian to the ground.

'Go, Cushla!' her father called, snapping his camera in a frenzy.

Stretch and Josh approached the crocodile's giant jaws with a roll of duct tape.

'Okay, team, we've got to work fast,' he told them. 'The less time we take, the less stress on old Super Croc here and the less stress on us as well.'

Stretch quickly secured both of the croc's jaws with duct tape. He then brought out a blindfold to calm the croc, securing it with tape. Stretch stood back as the scientist scrubbed an area on the crocodile's back between its nuchal scutes, and gave the croc an injection.

'What's he doing now?' Cushla whispered to Terri.

'Giving him a local anaesthetic,' Terri explained. 'He's going to drill small holes through the scutes – they're like scales – on the back of his neck so we can attach a satellite transmitter to him. Don't worry,' she added, when she caught sight of Cushla's face. 'The scutes are really thick and bony on that part of his body, and because of the injection, he won't feel a thing.'

'But why don't you just sedate him?' Cushla asked. 'Give him enough anaesthetic to knock him out altogether?'

'They mightn't look it but crocs are actually very fragile creatures,' Terri explained. 'They can't withstand sedatives like some other wild animals can. It's all to do with them being cold-blooded – they have a different metabolism to mammals.'

Cushla nodded. They'd just been studying metabolism and body temperatures in science at school. It was so much more interesting to find out what it meant in a real-life situation, rather than just read about it in a textbook.

'So that's why we just restrain them instead?' she asked Terri.

'You got it.'

After Stretch had finished drilling, he threaded pieces of speciallly-designed corrosive wire through the holes, then attached the satellite tracker. The tracker was dark green to help disguise it against the croc's scales. 'We don't want to interfere with the croc's ability to hunt prey,' Terri explained, 'or make it stand out to bigger croc, who might attack it.'

'But what's the satellite tracker for?' Cushla asked.

Terri grinned. 'I'm going to have to fill you in on that one later. Looks like we're getting ready to release him again!'

Josh and Avi, another team member, were carefully removing the blindfold and ropes. 'Easy does it,' Josh whispered as he pulled apart the last knot.

Cushla was instructed to jump off first before the croc was released. Super Croc had had enough of eight humans holding him down, and was eager to put as much distance between them and himself as possible. As soon as he saw the river, he scrambled across the flat, slid down the muddy bank and swam off to freedom.

Everyone in the croc team burst into applause. Another research mission successfully accomplished!

Cushla ran back to her parents, grinning broadly. 'Did you see me?' she cried, her legs still wobbly from the excitement of it all. 'Did you see me helping to hold down the crocodile?'

Her dad gave her a hug, and patted his camera. 'Sure did, Cushla. And I have the pictures in here to prove it!'

Later, after the sun had gone down, the McBrides and the Irwins sat around the flickering campfire, chatting about their day. Terri had mixed up a huge batch of damper to bake over the hot coals.

Stretch eased his lanky frame into the space beside Cushla and Bindi. 'Mind if I join you?' he asked.

Bindi smiled at him. 'Not at all. You did a great job with those ropes today.'

Stretch grinned. 'You didn't do too badly yourself, Miss Number One Croc-Jumper. You too, Cushla. Bet you don't have too many crocodiles back home in Ireland.'

Cushla shook her head. 'We don't even have any snakes!'

'None at all?' asked Robert. 'Too bad you don't have scrub pythons. I saw one today, B, while you guys were busy with Super Croc. It was huge! Must have been about six metres long, I reckon.' He held out his hands. 'Its head was *this* big.'

Cushla shuddered. She liked pretty much all animals, except for snakes. '*Definitely* not scrub pythons.' Eager to change the subject, she turned to Terri. 'So can you tell us more about the satellite transmitter now? What it's used for?'

'How about you tell the McBrides about our project, Stretch?' said Terry. 'You are the expert, after all.'

'Sure,' said Stretch, popping a piece of damper into his mouth and chewing on it thoughtfully. 'Up until a few years ago, we didn't know too much about the secret world of saltwater crocs. What they do, where they go, how long they spend there – that kind of thing. Salties aren't the easiest animal to study in the wild.'

'Too dangerous?' suggested Cushla's dad.

'Actually, they're surprisingly shy,' Stretch went on. 'They spend a lot of time underwater. We also use acoustic tags. They let us know where the croc is while it's in the river. However, it only tracks where the receivers are positioned. But you know that satellite transmitter we fitted today?'

Cushla nodded.

'It gives us more extensive information, as we can track the crocodile wherever it goes.'

'So it's all done from space?' Cushla asked. 'Amazing.'

'They put satellite trackers on all kinds of animals,' Bindi added. 'Turtles, dugongs – even great white sharks. Hey, Stretch, tell Cushla about Banana.'

'You put a satellite on a *banana*?' Cushla asked. 'What for? To find out where it went after it was picked?'

Robert laughed. 'Banana's a salty. My dad worked with him a few years back. After they put the tracker on him, they wrapped him up in a net and airlifted him by helicopter to a beach over 50 kilometres away from where he was caught, to see what he'd do.'

'You were there too, weren't you, Stretch?' Terri added.

'Sure was. He was a good little mover, Banana. He spent the first couple of weeks just moseying around up and down the coastline. We figured he was going to stay in his new home. Then the next thing he does is travel back up the coast and inland to the same pool where we trapped him.' Stretch stopped to take another bite of damper then continued the story.

'He travelled 50 kilometres in five days. Pretty fast, eh? The last three k's were overland through thick scrub. He proved to us that salties have a great homing instinct.'

'Sounds just like a homing pigeon,' remarked Cushla's dad. 'We used to have some of those when I was a boy.'

Stretch washed down the last of his damper with a gulp of billy tea, yawned and stretched, then stood up. 'Yep, crocs are amazing creatures, all right. See you all in the morning, okay?'

'Goodnight, Stretch,' everyone called as he headed off to his swag.

'Time for bed for us, too,' Terri announced. 'We've got a big day ahead of us in the morning.'

'Awww,' sighed Robert. 'Can't we have a few more stories? I love hearing about the big crocs Dad used to work with.'

'Maybe tomorrow.' Terri ruffled Robert's hair, then pointed him in the direction of their tent. 'Now, scoot. It's late.'

CHAPTER THREE

THE NEXT MORNING, EVERYONE
was up bright and early. Now that they'd had
their croc-jumping experience, the McBrides were
heading back to Brisbane to spend some more time
with their Australian relatives before flying home.

The Irwins were heading to the airport as well.
Only they weren't returning to Australia Zoo.

They were catching a small plane to Minyalwuy, a tiny settlement on the other side of the Gulf of Carpentaria, to visit family friends.

'I can't wait to see Charlie again,' Bindi told her mum as they packed their gear into the back of the Range Rover.

'Me too,' said Robert. 'Do you think Uncle Eddie will take us fishing?'

'Maybe,' said Terri, with a smile. 'It depends if he has any spare time.'

Eddie wasn't Bindi and Robert's real uncle – just an old friend of their dad's. They'd worked together years ago, and now Eddie was a sea ranger for the local Aboriginal Corporation. He helped to protect and care for the land and its creatures, as his ancestors had done for generations before him. And Charlie was his son. It was going to be

Charlie's fourteenth birthday in a few days' time, and, seeing as they were already in the Top End, the Irwins had decided to visit so they could help him to celebrate it.

Bindi's head was already full of party ideas. 'Maybe we should all dress up as movie stars, like we did for my 12th birthday party at Australia Zoo,' she suggested. 'Or we could have another 50's rock'n'roll party like we did last year. With lots of dancing and really awesome golden-oldie music.'

Robert wrinkled his nose. 'Hmmm. I'm not sure Charlie would go for either of those.'

'He's probably got his own ideas about what he wants to do for his party,' Terri agreed. 'He does like music though . . .' She broke off as she heard a loud whistle from above their heads.

'Look!' Bindi cried, pointing to a large black, red-cheeked bird hanging upside down from a nearby branch. 'It's a palm cockatoo. He's come to say hello.'

'Hel–lo!' squawked the bird, right on cue, making everyone laugh.

Cushla dropped the swag she'd been rolling up and stared at the bird, wide-eyed. 'Did someone train him to say that?' she asked the Irwins.

'It's just one of their natural calls,' Bindi told her. 'Amazing, isn't it? It really does sound like he's saying hello.'

'They've got another really awesome trick, too,' Robert said as the bird moved sideways along the branch and broke off a stick with its sharp beak. 'Look, B, he's going to play drums for us.'

Everyone watched, spellbound, as the cockatoo flew with the stick to a hollow tree branch, then began beating the stick against it.

'Maybe he's celebrating a birthday too,' Cushla suggested.

Bindi smiled. 'More likely there's another palm cockatoo in the area. A female one. He's trying to attract her attention with his musical display.'

Cushla sighed. 'I love this place. There are so many incredible animals here. A bird that plays drums, and crocodiles that can find their way home from miles away.' She blinked as a brilliantly coloured bird flitted past, a small lizard dangling from its beak. 'What was that?' she gasped.

'A yellow-billed kingfisher,' Robert told her.

'See?' Cushla said, marvelling at its bright blue and yellow feathers. 'None of our birds look like that, either.'

'I know,' Bindi said. 'The reserve is a really special place. And you've only seen a few of the creatures that live here. There are spotted cuscus, whiptail stingrays and rufous owls. I'm really going to miss it when we leave, too.'

'And the archerfish,' Robert pointed out. 'Don't forget them.'

'Archerfish?' Cushla said. 'Don't tell me, they can shoot a bow and arrow?'

'Don't be silly,' Robert giggled. 'They do shoot at insects though, except with jets of water.'

'Now you're having a lend of me,' Cushla laughed.

Robert stared at her, puzzled. 'A lend?'

'She means she thinks you're pulling her leg,' Terri translated for him.

'O-o-oh,' said Robert. 'I get it.' He put on his most serious face. 'But, fair dinkum, they do shoot jets of water at insects. It's how they catch their dinner. They fill their mouths with water then spit it high into the air, like this. *Pssshhhooo*!' He made a spitting motion with his mouth to demonstrate what he meant. 'The jet can knock a beetle off a twig a whole metre away. Then they eat it up. Chomp chomp.'

'Okay, Robert, I think Cushla gets the picture,' Terri laughed. She pulled Bindi in close for a hug. 'Don't worry, B,' her mother consoled her. 'We'll be back again next year. Someone's got to jump on old Super Croc again so we can change the batteries in his tracking device.'

Terri pushed the last of the gear into the back of the Range Rover, then jangled the keys. 'Okay, everyone, time to ship out. We've got places to be and planes to catch.' She squeezed Robert's shoulders. 'And we're not going to catch them if we stand around here spitting at beetles.'

CHAPTER FOUR

THE IRWINS' PLANE SKIDDED

to a halt on the tarmac, scattering a flock of birds. Bindi was the first through the airport doors. She'd never been to this part of the Northern Territory before, and was excited to check out its wildlife. She'd heard there were plenty of saltwater crocs in this part of the country, and was looking forward to some close encounters with them – maybe even some more croc-jumping!

'Welcome to Minyalwuy!' Eddie said warmly, pulling each family member into a hug while Charlie stood back, grinning broadly.

'Gee, Charlie, you must have grown a head taller since we last saw you,' Terri said, making him blush.

'Your kids have grown too,' Eddie told Terri, winking at Robert. He led them over to the luggage truck to collect their bags. 'Want me to carry anything for you?' he asked Bindi.

'No thanks, Eddie, I'm fine,' she replied, lifting her red canvas bag from the tray of the luggage truck. Bindi did so much travelling with her Wildlife Warrior and TV work, she had packing down to a fine art. Only the absolute essentials went into her bag.

The Irwins followed Eddie and Charlie out to the parking lot, where a sea of virtually identical white four-wheel drives sat waiting for their owners.

'How do you ever find your car?' Robert asked, shaking his head. 'They all look exactly the same.'

'Dad's is the dirtiest one,' Charlie laughed, pointing to their vehicle. It was almost completely covered in a coat of red dust.

'Yeah, sorry about that,' Eddie apologised. 'I had to go off-road this morning to check out a report of a distressed turtle at Rainbow Beach.'

'Poor thing,' sighed Bindi, her eyes softening with concern. 'Is he okay?'

'He is now,' Eddie assured her, opening the door of the boot so the Irwins could stow their luggage.

'But he was in pretty bad shape when I found him. His front flippers were cut up quite badly.'

'Just as well you were there to help him out,' said Bindi. Despite the many years she'd been working with animals, it always upset her to hear about ones that were in trouble or pain.

'The sea rangers do a great job,' Charlie said proudly. 'As soon as I finish school, I'm going to be one too.'

'Good for you,' said Terri. 'If you're anything like your dad, you'll be terrific.'

Twenty minutes later, Eddie pulled up in front of a low wooden building surrounded by gum trees. 'Charlie and I have a bit of shopping to do, so we'll meet you back here in half an hour, okay?' he explained to Terri and the kids. 'Lisa will help you out with your permit.'

'Thanks, Eddie,' said Terri. 'See you soon.'

While Terri filled out the paperwork for the permit that would allow the Irwins to travel on Aboriginal land, Bindi and Robert explored the office. The walls were crammed full of awards the rangers had won for their environmental work in the area.

'Check this one out,' Robert said, pointing to a glass pyramid. 'It's an award for managing yellow crazy ants.'

'Yellow crazy ants?' said a tall boy standing next to him. 'They sound kind of cool.'

Bindi turned and smiled at him. 'I'm not sure "cool" is the right word to describe them – especially if you got in their way.'

'Yeah? What do they do? Bite you?' The boy

scratched a small red lump on his arm. 'I got bitten by a bull ant the other day and it still hurts.'

Robert shook his head. 'They don't bite their prey. They spray formic acid on them instead. Then they swarm all over them.'

The boy flinched. 'Eew. I'll definitely be staying out of their way then. Is that why they call them "crazy"?'

Robert squished up his eyes. 'Not really. It's more because they jerk around in a frenzy if you disturb their nest. Like this!' he added, kicking his arms and legs out in a crazy dance as he demonstrated the movements for his new friend.

Bindi couldn't help but grin. She was just about to suggest he quieten down a bit when a large photo on the opposite wall caught her eye.

'Oh no,' she murmured, moving closer so she could see more clearly. 'The poor thing.'

The photo showed a giant net on the shoreline. Inside, completely entangled by criss-crossed twisting ropes, lay a turtle, its eyes dull and lifeless.

Robert and his new friend came over to join her, followed by a girl around Bindi's age. She had the same straw-blonde hair and crinkly blue eyes as the boy, and was obviously his sister.

'You okay, B?' asked Robert.

Bindi nodded, hoping this wasn't what had happened to the turtle Eddie had mentioned.

'How did it get in there?' the girl asked. 'It looks like someone's wrapped a tennis net around it and dumped it on the sand. How could anyone be so cruel?'

'How would a tennis net end up on the beach?' asked her brother.

Bindi moved even closer to the photo so she could get a better view of the net. She'd heard from Stretch about this kind of thing happening before, on the north-western beaches of Cape York, but she'd never actually seen it for herself. Some of the turtles the rangers had recovered had had to be airlifted back to the wildlife hospital at Australia Zoo to have their damaged flippers amputated. The turtles then spent months in rehabilitation before they could be released back into the wild.

'It's not a tennis net,' Bindi said slowly. 'It's a fishing net. The rangers call them ghost nets.'

'*Ghost* nets?' the boy laughed. 'Looks pretty real to me.'

He waggled his hands in his sister's face. 'I'm a

ghost net and I'm coming to get you,' he droned in a spooky voice, then made a howling sound.

'Cut it out, Ry,' the girl said, rolling her eyes. 'Don't be such an idiot.'

Bindi gave her a sympathetic smile, then looked over to the front counter, where her mum was busy checking out maps and chatting to a couple who she guessed must be the boy and girl's parents. Figuring her mum would be tied up for a while, Bindi turned back to the others.

'I know it sounds like a funny name,' she began, 'but the whole thing's actually pretty serious.' Bindi was just casting around in her mind for the best words to explain ghost nets to him when a tall woman, wearing a khaki uniform similar to Eddie's, appeared at her side.

'Everything okay here?' the woman asked.

'Fine, thanks,' Bindi assured her, hoping they hadn't been too noisy. 'I was just trying to explain to . . . um . . . this guy here –'

'His name's Ryan,' the girl said, giving her brother a killer stare. 'And I'm Samantha. Sam for short.'

'Thanks, Sam,' Bindi said. 'Um . . . nice to meet you guys.'

The tall woman smiled at her. 'Are you Bindi, by any chance?'

Bindi nodded, puzzled by the question.

'I'm Buduwutpuy, one of the sea rangers here,' the woman said, pointing to the name tag on her uniform. 'Though most people just call me Buddy. Eddie said your family would be dropping by sometime today.'

'We just flew in this morning,' Bindi said,

pushing her brother forward. 'This is Robert, and that's my mum, Terri, over there.' Bindi pointed to her mother, who was still deep in conversation with the couple at the counter.

She studied Buddy's name tag for a moment. It was always nice to meet someone else with an unusual name. 'Budu-wut-puy,' she said, pronouncing the word carefully. 'That's a really pretty name.'

'Thanks,' Buddy said, smiling. 'It means "fruit of the cycad plant". Cycads have been around since –'

'–the dinosaurs from the Jurassic period,' Robert said, finishing the sentence for her. 'That's over 200 million years ago.'

'Well, I'm not *quite* that old myself,' Buddy laughed. 'But yes, you're absolutely correct. Cycads are fern-like plants that have been around for millions of years, and were one of the main food sources for dinosaurs of that era.' She paused. 'So, what can I help you guys with? Looking for something to do while you're in the area?' She tapped a pile of leaflets on the wall display. 'We've got some great guided walks you could take, or you could go bird-watching. There are sea eagles, and –'

'We were just looking at this photo of the turtle trapped in the ghost net,' Bindi interrupted her. 'And I was trying to explain to Sam and Ryan what they are.'

'Right,' Buddy said thoughtfully. 'Okay, well, ghost nets are giant nets that have come from fishing boats operating in the South China Sea. Some of them may have accidentally been swept overboard, but most have simply been dumped in the ocean when they're too old and holey to properly catch fish anymore.

'And these nets just drift around in the ocean as though they're being guided by a "ghostly hand" – that's how they got their name – but it's really by the currents and tides. Trouble is, they pick up marine life as they go – not just fish, which they were designed to catch, but bigger animals as well.'

'Like turtles?' Sam asked, her voice catching as she looked at the photo again.

'Turtles, dugongs, dolphins, sharks, seabirds – even whales and crocodiles,' explained Buddy. 'The tides wash the ghost nets onshore all around the gulf. That's where we find them, often with several creatures still trapped inside.'

'How big do the nets get?' Ryan asked.

'Oh, big,' Buddy told him. '*Huge*. We heard from one of the rangers from down the coast that they'd found one that weighed as much as ten tonnes.'

Ryan tried to imagine how big ten tonnes was. 'You mean as big as a truck?'

'More, probably,' Robert said. 'Ten tonnes is about the same weight as two African elephants.'

Bindi shook her head, grinning. 'Trust you to know that, Robert.'

'The biggest net found around here was only six tonnes,' Buddy said. 'A storm blew it onto Britton Island last year, where it became stuck on coral. It was still too heavy for us to cut it free ourselves, though. We had to borrow some equipment from the local mine to help move it. Others we find are half-buried in the sand, and we have to dig them out.'

'Then what do you do with them?' asked Sam.

'If they're too heavy to lift, we push them further up the beach, away from the tideline. If we get a king tide, it might wash them out to sea again, and more creatures will be trapped.

'But mainly we cut them up and take them away in the back of a ute, then dump them in landfill – *after* we've rescued any trapped wildlife inside them,' she added quickly, when she saw the look of horror on Sam's face.

Bindi was just about to ask another question when Terri came over. 'Right,' she said cheerily, waving the permit at them, 'that's all organised then. You two ready to go? Eddie will be back soo–' She broke off as she took in everyone's long faces. 'Is something wrong?' she asked gently.

'Something is *definitely* wrong,' Bindi sighed,

shaking her head. 'I don't know how people can be so thoughtless. There must be something we can do.'

'Yeah,' Robert agreed. 'But what? We're only kids.'

CHAPTER FIVE

EDDIE'S HOUSE WAS SITUATED

at the back of the town, on the edge of the nature reserve. After a quick shower to freshen up after the morning's travels, the Irwins were treated to a tasty late lunch out on the veranda.

While they ate, Bindi and Robert kept an eye out for signs of wildlife in the bush on the other side of the road. Robert was hoping to see a northern quoll – a meat-eating marsupial that looks a bit like a cat. Since cane toads had invaded northern Australia, whole populations of northern quolls had been wiped out, and there were very few left in the wild.

'Seen any *barkuma* yet?' Eddie asked him, using his clan's name for the local quoll.

'Not sure,' admitted Robert. 'I thought I saw something moving through the bush over there, but it might just have been a wild dog.'

Marlena, Eddie's wife, nodded. 'Plenty of them about. Come back at night-time when the bins are out, and you'll see a whole mob of them sneaking around looking for a free feed.'

Bindi put down her sandwich and pointed towards another part of the reserve. 'Did you see that?'

Everyone's eyes followed her finger.

'Over there. Moving through the trees. It's really fast, whatever it is.'

'Where?' asked Robert, straining his neck to spot it.

'Over there near those big gums,' said Bindi. 'Look, it's stopped now. It's sitting up on its haunches, watching us.'

'I see it,' said Charlie. 'He's a nice one too.'

'Nice one what?!' said Robert, upset that he was missing out on all the action.

'*Dhum'thum*,' said Eddie. 'Agile wallaby. We get a few of them around here, but you have to be quick to see them in the daytime. They come out more around dusk to feed.'

Robert sat back in his chair, disappointed. 'I still can't see it.'

'Never mind,' Eddie told him. 'You'll see lots of different animals when we go over to Britton Island tomorrow in my boat. *Damala* – that's white-bellied sea eagles to you – and *gurrumattji* – they're magpie geese. They have bright red cheeks, you can't miss them.'

'How about crocodiles?' Robert asked, brightening up a little.

'*Baru*?' said Charlie. 'Sure. They're everywhere.' He turned to Bindi. 'You have to be really careful on the beaches around here,' he began, then stopped and blushed, remembering that Bindi had been around crocodiles nearly every day of her life. 'But I don't need to tell *you* that, do I?'

'Ah . . . no,' said Bindi, giving Charlie a playful shove. 'You certainly don't.'

Marlena stood up and began to clear the

table. 'Why don't you show Bindi your paintings, Charlie?' She nodded to her husband. 'He's a really talented artist, isn't he, Eddie?'

'That's for sure,' Charlie's father said proudly. 'Just like his grandmother, and her mother and aunties too.' He grinned. 'It must have skipped a generation with me though, eh, Charlie? Come on, show Bindi what you've been painting.'

Charlie blushed again, deeper this time. 'Maybe later,' he mumbled.

'Hey, I'd love to see your paintings,' Bindi said quickly. 'Where do you do them? In your room?'

'Out in the shed,' said Charlie.

'So let's go then,' said Bindi. 'I love art,' she assured him. 'I'm not that good at it myself, but my friend Alicia is amazing. Mum's going to get her to paint my portrait one day.'

She followed Charlie down to the bottom of the yard, where an old wooden shed was tucked away under some stringybarks. Inside, the shed had been set up as a studio. There were shelves laden with brushes and tubes of colourful paint, and finished paintings stacked against the walls. In the middle of the studio, an old wooden table held the piece Charlie was currently working on – a painting of a group of eight dolphins leaping joyfully in the ocean.

Bindi was amazed. 'This is gorgeous! I love the colours. Especially the silvery blues of the ocean.' She looked closely at the brushstrokes. 'How do you get the water to shimmer like that? It almost looks real.'

'It's a technique my grandmother taught me,' Charlie told her. 'But she's way better than me.

She has paintings in the gallery, up in town.' He pulled a painting of a mother and baby dolphin from a stack. 'See? This one has the shimmering water too. You know how the name of our town is Minyalwuy?'

Bindi nodded, intrigued.

'Well, Minyalwuy means "where water becomes smooth and calm". We believe that when a baby dolphin is born, the water becomes smooth and shimmering.'

'That's beautiful,' said Bindi, flipping through some of his other paintings. She recognised lots of other wildlife from the area – long-necked turtles, agile wallabies, antilopine wallaroos. But most of the paintings were of dolphins. 'Why so many dolphins?' she asked, turning to Charlie. 'Are they your favourite animal?'

Charlie thought for a moment, his face serious. 'I guess so. I think it's something about the way they move. *Mutjalanydjal*, we call them. They're so carefree, like they're always having fun.' He tapped the stack, then grinned. 'But as you can see, I like lots of other animals as well. It's why I want to be a ranger like my dad.'

'Are you sure?' asked Bindi. 'Don't get me wrong, I think being a ranger would be a wonderful job – they do such good work.' She flung out her arm, pointing to the piles of paintings around the room. 'But you're such an amazing artist, Charlie. Your work is way better than lots of stuff I've seen hanging in galleries. Wouldn't you like to go away to art school when you finish high school here, and learn more about painting and drawing?'

Charlie looked at Bindi as though she were

crazy. 'To the city, you mean. Lots of roads and traffic and concrete and noise. Why would I want to do that?'

'But you're so talented,' Bindi began. 'And it would be a great opportunity for you, to go out and see the world.'

'Maybe. But the beaches and the bush and the animals and birds around here are my world. That's all I need to be happy. And I don't need to go to the city to learn about painting from strangers. I can find that out right here from my family.'

He picked up a brush and began adding more paint to the canvas. Bindi sat watching him in silence for a while, thinking about his answer. She and Charlie were obviously very different people. Her Wildlife Warrior work took her all over the world – to exotic places such as Indonesia, Japan and deepest, darkest Africa. She loved travelling and meeting new people and finding out all about their customs and cultures, eating their food and learning new languages. Whereas Charlie seemed perfectly happy to stay in the small town he'd grown up in for the rest of his life.

But if that was what he wanted to do, she respected his decision. The important thing, she realised, was that whatever you choose to do in life, it should be something that makes you happy.

CHAPTER SIX

'OKAY, GUYS,' SAID MARLENA,
bustling about on the jetty. 'Let's see how we're
doing. Life jackets?'

'Check!' Charlie and Bindi called in
unison.

'Sunhats?'

'Check!'

'Sunscreen? You can get really burnt when you're out on a boat.'

'Check!'

'Picnic basket?'

'Check!'

'Food and drinks?'

'Check!'

Marlena wrinkled her forehead, trying to remember if there was anything else they could have forgotten. When nothing came to mind, she ordered everyone onto the boat. 'Okay, crew, let's go!'

'Britton Island, here we come!' Charlie yelled, neatly jumping down into his father's boat. The Irwins clambered in after him, followed by Marlena and, finally, Eddie, who'd stayed on the jetty to organise the ropes.

Once on board, Eddie powered up the motor, slipped the last rope and eased the boat out of the small harbour and into the open water. The island was only a short distance away – less than a forty-minute boat ride.

'Check out the beach over there,' Terri said as they sped towards it. 'It looks amazing.'

Bindi stared at the white sand, fringed with dark green vegetation, and lapped by white-capped pale green waves. The Top End had some of the most beautiful beaches in the world. No wonder Charlie was so content to spend the rest of his life here. She settled back in her seat to enjoy the ride, marvelling at a pair of white-bellied sea eagles soaring above her head.

'Dad!' Charlie's voice broke her reverie. 'Cut the engine. Quick!'

Bindi snapped to attention, her fingers automatically clasping her life jacket. 'Is something wrong?' she blurted, her eyes wide.

Charlie grinned. 'Sorry to give you a fright, Bindi. I just spotted something I thought you'd like to see.'

He pointed to a small pod of dolphins playing in the water a few metres from the boat. 'We needed to cut the engine in case we scared them off, or they came too close to the propellers.'

'Oh, wow,' breathed Bindi.

'Look!' said Robert, his eyes lighting up with excitement. 'There's a baby one!'

Everyone moved to the left-hand side of the boat to watch the dolphin family skimming through the water, slapping their tails in the air each time they dived under the surface.

'Pretty neat, eh?' said Charlie.

Bindi stared at the creatures, puzzled. The dolphins were definitely gorgeous. But there was something different about them. For starters, the shape of their head. It was round like a melon, with a heavy crease across the back of the neck, and there was no long 'beak' like the ones bottlenose dolphins have.

And secondly, the fin in the middle of their back was much shorter and stubbier than the fins of other dolphins. And thirdly . . .

Bindi turned to Charlie. 'Umm . . .'

'You're going to say something about the dolphins, aren't you?' said Charlie, his eyes twinkling. 'How they don't *look* like other dolphins.'

Bindi stared at him, amazed. 'How did you know?'

Charlie grinned. 'Because everybody who comes up here and sees them says that.'

'Oh,' laughed Bindi, pleased her eyes hadn't been playing tricks on her. 'Are they a new species or something?'

'Yep. They're called snubfin dolphins, because of that snubby little fin on their backs. They were only officially "discovered" around seven years ago, although they've obviously been around a lot longer than that.'

'You telling Bindi about our special dolphins?' Eddie said, sliding along the bench towards them. 'They're only found in northern Australian waters, you know. Around Minyalwuy, of course, and a few other pockets here and there.'

'He sure is. How many of them are there, do you think?'

'Around here, you mean?' Eddie asked. 'Snubfins tend to hang out in very close-knit family groups. There are ten in this group, including the new baby dolphin that Robert pointed out, and there's another family of six a bit further down the coast. And they're only the groups that have been documented – there may be others.'

'I meant all up,' Bindi said. 'I'm just trying to get an idea of how rare they are. You said there were "pockets" of snubfins. That doesn't sound like very many.'

Eddie scratched his chin, trying to remember. 'I think I heard Buddy saying the other day there were only about a thousand snubfins in existence, so they're quite rare, yes. Rare enough for them to have a high conservation priority, anyway. The females only give birth to a single calf every two or three years, so they're not replacing themselves very efficiently. It puts them at risk of dying out as a species, definitely.'

Bindi nodded. Those statistics sounded very similar to the birth rates of giant pandas, one of the most highly threatened species in the world, whose habitat was being swallowed up by human land clearing. However, things were beginning to look up for the giant panda now that successful breeding programs had been put in place by the Chinese.

She turned her attention back to the creatures in the bay, only metres away from their boat. Occasionally, one of them jumped out of the water but never very high. She thought back to some of the special tricks she'd seen other dolphins do – not just in theme parks, but out in the open water as well. 'They don't leap up out of the water or do flips and turns like bottlenose dolphins, do they?' she remarked to Eddie.

Eddie shook his head. 'No, they're not natural acrobats. They don't bow ride either.'

'Bow ride?' said Robert, who'd been listening to their exchange. 'I love it when dolphins do that!'

'Dolphins are smart, aren't they?' Eddie laughed. 'Hitching a free ride from the wave the bow makes as the boat moves through the water – that takes real brain power.' He paused, trying to think of a good comparison. 'It's like when you go bodysurfing. The wave powers you all the way into shore, right?'

Robert nodded. 'It sure does.'

'Bow riding is like that for a dolphin. It makes it

easier for them to swim. They can cruise along with a boat for ages – it's less tiring for them.'

'And fun too, I reckon,' Charlie added. 'Who wouldn't want to go bow riding if they could?'

Bindi and Robert gazed out at the snubfins as their boat drifted gently with the currents. Bow riders or not, they were still incredibly cute and entertaining.

Robert tapped Bindi's arm. 'Hey, did you see that?'

'Depends,' Bindi replied, hiding a smile. 'What did you see?'

Robert pointed to a dolphin on the outer edge of the group. 'That guy just spat water in the air. Look – now they're all doing it!'

Bindi watched, entranced, as the rest of the

snubfins formed a circle, then held the top part of their bodies motionless above the surface, like a human treading water. They reminded her of whales when they 'spyhop' by raising their heads out of the water to check out what's going on above.

Each snubfin spat a stream of water high into the air.

'It's just like those archerfish back on the reserve,' Robert said. 'Except I don't think these guys are after insects.'

'Definitely not,' laughed Eddie. 'They're fishing.'

'*Fishing*?!' said Robert. 'How does that work?'

'You won't be able to see them from here,' Eddie told him, 'but the snubfins weren't just cruising around aimlessly before, they were chasing fish to the surface. Now they're working together, spitting jets of water at the fish to herd them towards each other so they can catch and eat them.'

'That's really clever,' said Bindi. She was always amazed by how smart animals could be, especially ones that worked together to achieve something that was beneficial to the whole group.

Eddie stood up and moved towards the control panel. 'Seen enough? If we don't get moving soon, the sun will be setting before we even get the picnic basket open,' he joked. 'And there's plenty of other interesting things to see over on the island.'

Reluctantly, Bindi nodded. She would quite happily watch the snubfins play and hunt all day if she could. No wonder Charlie enjoyed painting them so much. They were truly beautiful animals.

CHAPTER SEVEN

'ARE YOU READY, BINDI?' CALLED
Charlie. 'Jonah's here.'

Bindi grabbed her bag and followed Charlie out to the street, where his cousin Jonah was waiting to drive them to the surf lifesaving club.

'Thanks for the lift, mate,' said Charlie, as he and Bindi climbed inside.

Jonah grinned as he pulled away from the kerb. 'No worries, I had to go down to the club this evening anyway, so it was no hassle to pick you up on the way.' He smiled at Bindi. 'So you must be Bindi, yeah? Charlie's been talking about your visit for weeks.'

'Have not!' Charlie groaned, blushing. 'Don't listen to him, B. He's always making up stuff.' He turned back to Jonah, eager to change the subject. 'How are those nippers going? You keeping them out of mischief?'

'Barely,' Jonah laughed. 'They're always wanting to do the opposite of what they're supposed to do. Just as well Gav's there to help me keep them under control.'

'Gav is Jonah's older brother,' Charlie explained to Bindi. 'He's got kids of his own, which helps him anticipate what some of the others might do. He gets them all to run up and down the beach for the first half hour to tire them out a bit.'

'It works, too,' said Jonah. '*Most* of the time. And if it doesn't, we send them out on a paddleboard for another half an hour. *That* really tires them out.'

'I bet they love it,' said Bindi. Lots of her friends back home were nippers. They really enjoyed the activities the club put on for them, as well as the opportunity to learn how to stay safe in the water.

'So, Charlie,' said Jonah, changing the topic. 'You've got a big birthday bash coming up soon, I hear?'

'Yep,' Charlie said, nodding. 'That's what Jimi and the rest of the guys in his band are going to talk through tonight. We're going to work out what songs they're going to play at the party.'

'Ones you can dance to, I hope,' said Bindi.

'Definitely!' said Charlie, lighting up. 'Jimi's band is wicked. You're going to love it.'

'What's it called?' asked Bindi.

'He just told you,' said Jonah, a cheesy grin on his face.

'He did?' She turned towards Charlie, puzzled. 'I don't remember you saying anything about the band's name.'

Charlie and Jonah stared straight ahead for a moment, then burst out laughing. 'Should we tell her?' asked Jonah.

'Tell me what?' asked Bindi.

'I don't know,' said Charlie, shaking his head. 'It's wicked.'

'*What's* wicked?' Bindi cried, looking from one to the other, completely confused.

Then she slapped her forehead with the palm of her hand. 'Ooh,' she said, embarrassed it had taken her so long to work out. She was usually pretty quick with word games. 'I get it. The band's *name* is Wicked with a capital "w".'

'Yep!' said Charlie, winking at Jonah.

'Wic-ked,' drawled Jonah in his best DJ voice, making them all laugh. He hummed a little tune for a while, then turned to Charlie. 'How old are you going to be, Chaz? Fourteen?'

Charlie nodded.

'You'll be able to join the cadets then, if you want to,' Jonah went on. 'Get your Bronze Medallion and your Surf Rescue Certificate.' He grinned. 'Then you could help out Gav and me with the nippers. The three of us on the job would be deadly!'

'Maybe,' Charlie said. Helping out with the nippers sounded like fun, but it would take up time he wanted to spend on his painting. Eventually he wanted to be good enough to have some of his own paintings in the local gallery, alongside his grandmother's. 'Thanks for the lift, Jonah.'

'I'll see you guys back here in an hour or so, okay?'

Bindi gave him the thumbs up. 'See you then!'

'Hey, girl, where are you off to?' Bindi said, as a stocky blue heeler trotted past her on their way to the clubhouse.

'Hey, it's Bella,' said Charlie. He gave a low whistle and the dog bounded over and sat in front of him, then nudged his hand with her head. 'You're after a pat, aren't you, Bella?' cooed Charlie, running his fingers through the fur around her collar. The dog thumped her tail a few times in reply, then nudged Charlie's hand again.

'Do you think she'd let me pat her too?' Bindi asked.

'Sure,' said Charlie. 'She's really friendly.'

Bindi presented her hand, palm down, for the dog to sniff first. No matter how friendly a dog looked, she'd been taught it was always wise to do this before you tried to pat it, just in case it decided to take a snap at you instead. Once Bella had established Bindi was someone she could trust, she lay down on the ground and rolled over, exposing her belly.

'Ooh, you *really* like pats, don't you?' Bindi laughed, giving Bella's tummy a good rub.

Another whistle came from further along the beach. Bella's ears pricked up before she hastily scrambled back onto all fours and raced off across the sand to the water's edge.

'What a beautiful dog!' said Bindi, as she watched Bella chase a ball an old guy had thrown into the waves for her.

Charlie nodded. 'The best. Everyone loves Bella. She's a lifesaver, you know.'

'Why?' Bindi laughed. She wasn't going to fall for Charlie's word tricks twice in a row. 'Let me guess. Because she hangs out at the surf lifesaving club?'

'No,' Charlie said. 'Because she actually saved someone's life.'

'Who?' asked Bindi.

'Old Mick, her owner,' Charlie explained. 'That's

him down there on the beach with her. He's lucky to be alive.'

'Really?' said Bindi, intrigued. 'What happened?'

'Old Mick's the caretaker at the club. He lives – *used* to live – in an old house behind it. Then one day, he came home from work and let Bella off her chain so she could go for a swim, like he did every day. Only that day, he'd noticed there were a couple of wild dogs roaming the beach. He was worried Bella might get into a fight with them and get hurt, so he brought her inside instead.'

'The dogs didn't try to attack *him*, did they?' Bindi asked. 'Before he could get inside? Is that what happened? And then Bella fought them off?'

'It *could* have happened that way,' Charlie admitted. 'Blue heelers are very protective of their owners. But no, that's not what happened. He was in his bathroom, just about to climb into the shower, when Bella started barking really loudly. Not just a normal kind of loud – she was really going off, howling and hurling herself against the bathroom door.'

Bindi tried to think what might make a dog behave like that. Some kind of danger, that was for sure. 'Was someone trying to break into his house?'

Charlie shook his head. 'No. The kitchen was on fire! By this time, old Mick could see smoke coming in from under the bathroom door. He raced out, picked up Bella, and got out of the house fast. Five minutes later – *KABOOM!* – the whole place went up. Old Mick was lucky to be alive. If it hadn't been for Bella . . .'

'Just as well she didn't get her swim that day,' said Bindi, watching the dog bounding joyfully through the waves.

'That's for sure,' said Charlie. 'Anyway, enough about Bella. Come and meet my mates.'

Bindi followed Charlie up a set of steps to a shady area in front of the clubhouse, where a small group of teenagers sat drinking Cokes.

'Jimi, Rocky, Nessa – this is my friend Bindi,' said Charlie, introducing her to each of them in turn. 'Bindi and her family are up for my party.'

Nessa's face lit up in a smile. 'Hi Bindi. Great to meet you. Where are you from?'

'Queensland,' Bindi told her. 'Near the Sunshine Coast.'

'You look really familiar,' said Nessa. 'Have you been up here before?'

Bindi shook her head. 'First time. I really love it up here though.'

Nessa's eyes narrowed. 'That's strange. I *know* I've seen you before somewhere.'

Charlie grinned. 'Maybe you've seen her on TV? On that show, you know – *Bindi's Bootcamp*?'

Nessa blushed. 'Of course! My little sister and I used to watch your show every week. Now you're going to think I'm really silly.'

'Of course I don't,' Bindi reassured her. 'Don't worry about it.' She smiled, eager to take the attention off herself. 'So you're in the band that's going to be playing at Charlie's party?'

Nessa nodded.

'That's fantastic,' said Bindi. 'I wish I was good at music. What do you play?'

'Drums,' Nessa said proudly. 'And Jimi here

plays guitar,' she added, patting his arm. 'Rocky's our bass player.'

'Rocky's brothers are in the band as well,' Charlie cut in. 'His brother Aaron is the lead singer. And Sam plays *yidaki*, along with a few other instruments.'

'*Yidaki*?' Bindi repeated. 'What's that?'

'You'd call it a didgeridoo,' Rocky explained. 'It's the same thing. *Yidaki* is our name for it.'

'Sounds great,' said Bindi. 'I can't wait to hear you guys play. I really hope you do requests!'

'Wicked can play anything,' Jimi boasted. 'If you can hum it, we can play it.'

Nessa laughed. 'You'd better hope Bindi doesn't hold you to that,' she told Jimi. She stood up from the table, smoothing down her top. 'Come on,

Bindi. Let's leave these guys to their big talk and go for a walk along the beach. I want to hear *all* about your life at Australia Zoo!'

CHAPTER EIGHT

MARLENA TAPPED LIGHTLY ON
the guest bedroom door. 'Bindi? Are you awake?'

Bindi rolled over and stretched, then looked at the alarm clock beside her bed. *Crikey! Was that really the time?* Bindi hardly ever slept in – there was always so much to do every day, she never wanted to waste a minute of it. The beds her mother and brother were sleeping in were empty – they were obviously already up and about.

'Won't be a minute, Marlena,' called Bindi, shrugging a bathrobe on over her pyjamas. Now everyone would think she was a real sleepyhead! After a pizza with Charlie's mates at the surf lifesaving club, she and Charlie had sat up until late the night before, talking about everything from her work with endangered animals around the world to his dreams of having his own art exhibition one day. The hours had simply flown by. By the time she'd finally crept into bed, everyone else in the house was sound asleep.

Bindi showered and changed at lightning speed. She hurried into the kitchen to find Marlena sitting at the table, a pile of papers spread out before her.

'Where's everyone else?' asked Bindi.

Marlena looked up from her paperwork and smiled. 'Good morning. Your mum and Robert have gone for a walk to the lagoon to see if they can get some photos of the birds there,' Marlena told her. 'There are hundreds of different kinds, so I imagine they'll be a while. And Charlie's gone off on patrol with his dad. He thought you might like to go along too, but when you didn't come in with the others for breakfast . . .'

'You mean they've gone without me?' wailed Bindi, annoyed with herself for sleeping in. Now what was she going to do for the rest of the day?

Marlena smiled. 'Don't worry,' she reassured Bindi. 'They won't have gone far yet. Eddie just phoned to say they're over at Crocodile Creek, if you want to join them.'

'Crocodile Creek?' said Bindi, perking up

immediately. That sounded like her kind of place! She wondered if the rangers needed any help with croc-jumping. 'Is it far? Can I walk there from here?'

'Not unless you're an Olympic champion,' Marlena laughed. 'And even then it might be a bit tricky.' She pulled the scattered papers into a neat pile and stood up. 'Come on, jump in the car,' she said, throwing Bindi an apple and a banana from the fruit bowl on the kitchen bench. 'You can eat these on the way.'

Marlena drove along the coastal road until she spotted Eddie's four-wheel drive in a clearing. 'They'll be down that way,' she said, pointing to a dirt track that led down to the beach.

'Tell Charlie to make sure he stays out of trouble, okay?'

Bindi grinned. 'Will do. Thanks for the lift, Marlena!'

As soon as she reached the sandy shore, Bindi kicked off her shoes and ran to join Eddie and Charlie. The sun was already quite high in the sky, and the air was sticky and warm. She was glad she'd remembered to bring her hat.

Eddie and Charlie were working their way along the creek that flowed into the ocean, taking care not to trip over the roots of the mangroves that lined the banks. Bindi put her shoes back on, and fell into step beside them.

'Morning, Bindi,' Eddie said, his voice low. 'So you finally woke up then?'

'Robert said you were snoring so loudly he had

to get up early just so he could get some peace and quiet,' Charlie joked, then yelped as Bindi playfully punched him on the arm.

'I was *not*,' she insisted. 'If anyone snores in our family, it's Robert. Honestly, he sounds like a walrus with a cold sometimes.'

Eddie put his finger to his lips. 'Ssshhhh, you two, or I'll send you both back to the car.'

'Sorry,' Bindi whispered meekly as a pair of magpie geese rose out of the bushes and flapped away into the distance. She hoped her joking around hadn't disturbed them.

Eddie stopped, crouching down as he pointed out a slide mark on the muddy bank. 'A croc's been along here recently,' he said quietly. 'A big one by the look of it.'

'Maybe she's in the water right now,' Charlie whispered. 'Watching us.'

'Maybe she is,' Eddie whispered back.

Bindi scanned the green water for a giant pair of eyes and the top of a scaly head, but saw nothing. 'Are you planning to trap her?' she asked. 'So you can tag her?'

Eddie shook his head. 'We don't trap or tag crocs around here.'

'You don't?' said Bindi, puzzled. 'But it's such a great way to find out more about their behaviour so we can help to protect them.'

Eddie shook his head. 'I understand what you're saying. But crocodiles are important in a different way to the people who come from around here. Every clan group has a particular native animal as their ancestral totem. Ours is *baru* – the saltwater crocodile. We honour and respect it, and leave it alone to live its own life.'

Once again, Bindi realised there could be different ways of looking at things. And there wasn't *one* right way – one person's beliefs weren't any more right or important than another's. Eddie wasn't telling her it was wrong to tag crocodiles to find out more about them, rather, that it wasn't something his own people would do because it went against their beliefs. Just as there was no way Stretch or any other members of the croc team would tell Eddie how to do his job. Each party had too much respect for the other's way of thinking.

'So what have you come here to –' Bindi began, then broke off as she spied a mound of leaves and soil several metres away. Her eyes widened. 'Is that a crocodile nest?' she whispered to Eddie.

'Sure is,' he said. 'And the eggs are just about due to hatch. I've been watching this nest for a while now. From a respectful distance, of course,' he added. 'I wouldn't want to upset the mother crocodile.'

Bindi nodded, wondering what her own family's totem animal might be if they could choose one. Probably the same as Eddie's, she mused, remembering how much her dad had loved working with crocodiles. It was almost like he'd shared a special understanding with them.

She leaned forward, trying to get a better view of the nest. 'Looks like there are about fifty eggs in there.'

'At least fifty,' replied Eddie. 'The hatchlings will call to Mama Croc to let her know they're ready to come out of their eggs. She'll dig them up and carry them down to the water in her mouth. If any of the hatchlings are having trouble getting out of their shells, she'll help them out by rolling the eggs inside her mouth and gently squeezing them until they hatch.'

'Aren't crocodiles clever?' remarked Bindi. 'When you think of how sharp their teeth are, it's amazing how gentle the mothers can be.'

Eddie held his finger to his lips again, then stood up slowly. 'Mama Croc will be along any minute now,' he whispered, 'and she won't be too keen on meeting anyone she thinks might hurt or disturb her babies. Time for us to go.'

Slowly and carefully, he led Charlie and Bindi back through the twisting mangrove roots and onto the main beach.

CHAPTER NINE

EDDIE PULLED OUT OF THE
clearing and headed south.

'Where are we off to now?' asked Bindi.

'Turtle Bay. It's a secluded beach fringed by sand dunes about 20 k's down the coast road. Someone called the office just before to report they'd seen a large ghost net washed up on the beach. I need to check there's nothing trapped inside.'

Bindi's heart skipped a beat. With any luck the net would be empty, and all she'd have to do was wait with Eddie until another crew arrived to roll it up and take it away. Or, if it was too big, drag it further up the beach, away from the shoreline. But if it wasn't empty, and there were turtles trapped inside . . . She shivered at the thought.

Earlier in the year, Bindi had spent a week swimming and diving with green turtles on a tiny coral island on the Great Barrier Reef. She'd even climbed out of her warm bed in the middle of the night to watch a mother turtle lumbering out of the ocean and up the beach to lay her cargo of eggs in the sand. It had been one of the most amazing experiences of her life. So she wasn't sure she could

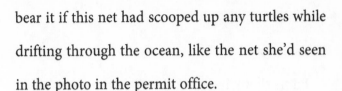

bear it if this net had scooped up any turtles while drifting through the ocean, like the net she'd seen in the photo in the permit office.

Eddie parked the car under a stand of casuarinas, and the three of them headed down to the beach. It didn't take them long to spot the ghost net, sprawled across the sand near a small pile of rocks. It was enormous – at least three tonnes, its thick strands tangled together like a giant ball of wool.

Bindi watched as Eddie walked around the perimeter of the net, lifting pieces here and there to check for signs of trapped wildlife. When she saw his shoulders slump, she knew he'd found something.

'Charlie?' Eddie called. 'Come here and give me a hand?'

'Turtle?' Charlie called back.

Eddie nodded, his face drawn.

'Is it okay?'

Eddie shook his head. 'Not this time, son.'

Taking a deep breath, Bindi followed Charlie to the spot where Eddie was crouching in the sand. She watched as he used a sharp knife to cut away thick strands of net to free the remains of a sea turtle, now only shell and bone.

'This one's been in here a long time,' sighed Eddie. 'I'd say the net has been drifting around the gulf for years, with the big monsoonal winds blowing it up onto different beaches. This is why we need to get rid of ghost nets altogether – to stop them at their source so this tragedy doesn't happen over and over again.'

Reaching into his pocket, he pulled out a notepad and pen, and began writing.

'Dad, what are you doing?' asked Charlie.

'Writing down all the details about the colour, size and shape of the strands of twine in the net. It's important to identify where the nets were made and which countries the fishing boats that use them come from. Once we know that, we let the government officials here know so they can take steps to fix the problem.

'Looks like anything they do will be too late for this little guy though,' he added, shaking his head.

Her eyes welling at the thought of the poor turtle thrashing about in its desperate efforts to escape, Bindi moved away from the net to a clear part of the beach. She kicked a piece of rubbery seaweed, sending it flying. It seemed so unfair.

Sea turtles could live for a long time, with several species living for at least fifty years – some even reaching a century!

But Bindi couldn't stay away for long. There could be other trapped wildlife that it wasn't too late to help. She moved around to the other side of the net from where Eddie and Charlie were working, inspecting each section carefully for any signs of movement.

Everything looked fine. Relieved, Bindi was about to rejoin Eddie and Charlie when something caught her eye. A large grey mass that was almost totally obscured by orange mesh and clumps of seaweed. A grey mass with a small, snubby fin in the middle of its back.

Bindi's heart sank. 'Eddie!' she called. 'You have to come here now!'

Hearing her cry, Eddie put down his knife and rushed over with Charlie close behind him.

'It's a dolphin, isn't it?' Bindi said, choking back tears. 'A snubfin.'

Eddie nodded. 'I'm afraid so. Poor little fella. It's only a young one, going by its size.'

A terrible thought occurred to Bindi. 'You don't think . . . It's not one of the dolphins from that family we saw on the way over to the island, is it?'

'Probably not,' Eddie reasoned. 'I think this one's been in the net for a while. Not as long as the turtle, obviously, but looking at its condition, a few days at least.'

He pointed to a series of lacerations on either side of the snubfin's body. 'You can see where it strained against the mesh, trying to work its way out.'

'Except it didn't make it,' Bindi said sadly. Eddie had told her snubfins lived in close-knit family groups, so somewhere out there a mother dolphin was probably swimming in search of her baby.

'What will happen to it now?' Bindi asked, her voice catching. 'Do you need me to –'

'I'll call one of the other rangers to come and help me retrieve the body,' Eddie reassured her, his voice soft. 'You don't need to worry about it anymore. Why don't you and Charlie go for a walk along the dunes for a bit? Check out some of our wonderful birdlife?'

'Sounds like a good idea,' said Charlie. His dad was right. They needed to spend some time with living things. 'Come on, Bindi,' he said, giving her a nudge. He pointed to a rock formation a few hundred metres along the shore. 'We'll head up that way, okay? See if there are any whistling kites?'

Bindi hesitated. Part of her wanted to get away from the scene that was making her feel so sad. But the part that made her a Wildlife Warrior was determined to stay exactly where she was. She was just about to tell Charlie her decision when a movement caught her eye. 'Did you see that?' she asked.

Charlie spun around. 'What?'

'Over there, right in the middle of the net. Something's moving.'

Charlie eyes followed her pointing finger. 'You're right!' he cried. 'There *is* something there. And it's still alive!' He turned and called to Eddie, who'd moved away from the net to make a call on his mobile. 'Hey, Dad! You better get back here now!' Then he carefully picked his way across the net.

Eddie flipped his phone shut. 'What is it?' he called, scrambling across the net to join his son. 'Another dolphin? Or a turtle?'

'A turtle,' Charlie said. 'Looks like a hawksbill. His front flippers are cut up pretty bad, but otherwise, he's okay, I think.'

Moving slowly and carefully, Bindi made her way over to them. She blanched when she saw how deep the cuts on the turtle's flippers were – almost through to the bone in places. This wasn't the first time she'd helped out a turtle in distress, she reminded herself. Although last time it had been a tiny plastic bag and a small length of fishing line, rather than a giant fishing net, threatening a turtle's life. The poor thing obviously needed help, and she resolved to do everything she could to provide it.

Working as quickly as he could, Eddie began to cut away strands of net from around the turtle's body. 'Looks like we might have got here just in time,' he said. 'Another few hours out of the water and under the hot sun like this . . . I don't think he would have lasted much longer.'

'He's pretty quiet,' said Charlie. He'd been expecting the turtle to thrash around upon their approach, but so far it had remained still.

'He's probably exhausted,' Eddie replied. 'You would be too, if you'd been through the same ordeal. When he first swam into the net, he would have panicked a fair bit while trying to escape. Then, in his struggle to break free, he probably just made things worse for himself, tangling himself up tighter and tighter.'

'I think he knows we're trying to help him,' Bindi said, reaching out a careful finger to stroke the turtle's shell through the crisscross of mesh. 'Don't worry, little one. We'll have you all patched up and back in the water as soon as we can.'

Eddie put down his knife for a moment and smiled, a faraway look in his eyes. 'You sound more and more like your dad every day, Bindi.'

Bindi's cheeks flushed. 'Do I?'

'Yep,' Eddie said, picking up his knife again so he could sort out a particularly difficult knot. 'When we worked together, he used to talk to animals just like that. Maybe it's *you* keeping our patient calm.'

'Bindi, the turtle whisperer,' Charlie laughed. 'Wait till I tell my mates your new name.'

'Sounds great! I'd even tell them myself,' Bindi said cheekily, sticking her tongue out at him.

Then she reached across and gave the turtle another gentle pat, feeling some of the sadness she'd felt earlier for the young dolphin lift and float away. At least they'd been able to help one of the animals they'd encountered that morning.

But in her heart of hearts, Bindi knew it wasn't enough. And though he'd gone back to his annoying habit of cracking silly jokes, she could tell by the look in Charlie's eyes that he felt exactly the same way.

CHAPTER TEN

BINDI STOOD IN FRONT OF THE
bathroom mirror, admiring the new hairstyle
Nessa had just given her for Charlie's party that
night. When she was working at Australia Zoo or
out in the field, she usually just pulled her hair into
a ponytail, or twisted it into a thick plait, with her
hat shoved on top. But Nessa had brought over her

curling wand, and now a tumble of curls cascaded down Bindi's back.

'Okay, now for some blush,' Nessa said, sweeping a thick brush across Bindi's cheekbones.

'Hey, that tickles!' Bindi laughed.

'Keep still,' Nessa ordered, 'or you'll end up with it all over your face.' Grabbing a soft pink lipstick from her make-up bag, she expertly outlined Bindi's lips. 'Now, smack them together gently like this,' she instructed, demonstrating what to do.

'Mwah!' said Bindi, pouting her lips. 'Is that how you do it? What's next?'

Nessa held up a mascara wand.

'Uh-uh,' said Bindi, swatting Nessa's hand away. 'None of that, thank you very much. I don't want to have to worry about my mascara running.'

Nessa rolled her eyes. 'This mascara is waterproof.'

Bindi wrinkled her nose. 'Still don't want any, thanks.'

'You're lucky,' Nessa sighed. 'You don't need it anyway. You've got really long eyelashes.'

'Robert reckons my eyelashes look like a giraffe's,' Bindi said, shaking her head.

'Better than having ones like a monkey,' Nessa laughed.

'Or a b-b-b-baboon,' Bindi said, exploding into a fit of giggles. Nessa was fun, she decided. Charlie was great to hang out with too, but it felt good to have some girl time for a change. She was missing her besties.

'So what do you think of my dress?' she asked Nessa, doing a little twirl in front of the mirror. 'Mum got it for me especially for the party.'

'It's really pretty,' Nessa said, admiring its delicate pattern. She was wearing a sparkly crop top and black jeans. Dresses weren't very practical for playing the drums in.

Terri appeared at the bathroom door. 'All set to go, girls?' she asked, her eyes dancing. 'Eddie said to let you know he's leaving in exactly two minutes.'

'You bet!' said Bindi, checking her reflection in the bathroom mirror one last time before heading out the door.

'You look great, Bindi,' said Jimi, as they helped load Nessa's drums out of her dad's ute and onto the makeshift stage at the surf lifesaving club.

'Hey, thanks,' said Bindi, suddenly shy. 'Are many people coming tonight, do you think?'

'What do you mean?' Jimi joked. 'Wicked are playing. *Everyone* will be here!'

'Just family and friends, actually,' Charlie corrected him.

'That *is* practically everyone,' Nessa laughed. 'Charlie's related to just about every person in town.'

'It's not a very big town,' Charlie pointed out.

'Just as well,' said Nessa, looking at the line of people streaming through the door, 'or you'd need to hire a bigger venue.'

'So where did you disappear to this afternoon?' Bindi asked Charlie, once everything was in place on the stage. 'I came looking for you, but I couldn't find you anywhere. Even your shed was all locked up.'

'Just around,' Charlie said mysteriously. 'Come on, this is supposed to be my party, not Twenty Questions. Let's go and get some food.'

Ten minutes later, the band started up and everyone in the room jumped up to dance. Even Old Mick, the caretaker, did a lap of the room with Bella in his arms. Jonah and Charlie had been absolutely right – Wicked were wicked! Every song they played had an amazing beat you couldn't help moving to. By the time they'd finished the first set, Bindi was almost out of breath.

Nessa jumped down from the stage to join her, her eyes shining. 'Well? What do you think? Are we any good?'

'You guys are better than good,' Bindi assured her. 'You were great! Can I book you for my next birthday party? It's coming up next month.'

'No worries,' Nessa laughed. 'We'll all cruise over to your place in our dolphin-powered submarine.'

Bindi bit her lip. The music and dancing and all the fun of getting ready with Nessa had helped her to push the sad thoughts about the trapped snubfin to the back of her mind. But now she felt all the joy emptying out of her body again.

'Oh, sorry, Bindi,' Nessa murmured, pulling her into a hug. 'Me and my big mouth. Charlie told me about you guys finding the snubfin on the beach yesterday. It must have been awful.'

'It was just a baby,' Bindi told her. 'And it was such a horrible way for it to die. There has to be something we can do to stop this from happening again.'

Charlie appeared beside them with a glass of juice. 'This is for you,' he said, passing it to Nessa.

'You must be thirsty after all that drumming. You guys are smashing it tonight.'

'Thanks, Charlie,' Nessa said. 'Glad you're enjoying it.'

Charlie turned to Bindi. 'Sorry, I should have brought one over for you as well.' His cheerful expression changed when he saw her face. 'Hey, are you okay?'

'She's upset about the snubfin,' Nessa explained.

'Sorry, Charlie,' Bindi said. 'This is your birthday party. You should be enjoying yourself with your friends, not worrying about me.'

'You're my friend, too, remember?' Charlie said, putting a hand on her shoulder. 'And don't worry, I've been thinking about that ghost net all day. There must be something we can do.'

'I know,' replied Bindi, her voice catching. 'I was just saying the same thing to Nessa.'

'But what, though?' Nessa asked. 'Dad says they're everywhere – hundreds of them – all over the beaches around here. And we're just kids. What can *we* do?'

'I don't know yet. Let's go and sit over there and we'll work on a plan,' Charlie said, pointing to a group of empty seats on the lawn. 'I'll get Jonah and Gav to come over. They've always got good ideas.'

'Grab Jimi and Rocky too,' Nessa suggested. 'And Rocky's brothers.' She gave Bindi another hug. 'Don't worry, B. We'll sort it out. We're –'

'Wicked!' Bindi chimed in, giving Nessa a high five.

CHAPTER ELEVEN

'ARE YOU *SURE* YOUR PARENTS
don't mind us using their caravan as our base?'
Bindi asked Nessa for the fifth time that morning.

'Are you kidding?' Nessa laughed. 'It's the
school holidays. They're just happy I'm outside
doing something useful instead of sitting in front
of the TV or computer all day.'

It had only taken Charlie's friends half an hour to come up with a brilliant plan. They'd decided to organise a public volunteer event to remove any ghost nets found in the area. All the volunteers who signed up for the program would be placed in teams big enough to move even the heavyweight nets so there would be no chance of them ever coming back on another high tide.

But they weren't only going to get rid of ghost nets. During the meeting, Jonah had suggested they collect marine debris as well. He was sick of stepping over plastic bottles and old rubber thongs every time he took his dog for a walk on the beach. Like the ghost nets, the currents and tides swept the marine debris in a clockwise direction around the gulf until it ended up on the beaches of Minyalwuy. Their once pristine beaches were turning into open-air garbage dumps.

Once they'd come up with their plan – which they'd named 'Project Wicked', of course! – the team had had to work quickly to put it into action. The Irwins would only be in town for a few more days, and Bindi was determined to be there for the event.

And now the day had finally arrived. Kids of all ages were already beginning to turn up to the marshalling areas to collect their Project Wicked kits. Each pack contained green garbage bags and a pair of rubber gloves the local supermarket had kindly donated to the cause.

Bindi ushered all the key players into the caravan for a final briefing.

'Okay,' she said, consulting her list. 'Jonah?

You and Gav have both got driver's licences, so I've put you in charge of all the people with utes. You need to make sure they're at the right beaches when needed and know what do with the nets once they're loaded up.'

'Take them to the tip, right?' said Gav.

'Exactly,' Bindi said. 'Next. Aaron and Sam? You're in charge of the marine debris weighing stations. We've set up a few for different types of rubbish. Plastic bottles can be recycled, so they'll have their own station. Most other stuff, like thongs or cigarette lighters, will end up in the tip with the ghost nets.'

'What about big stuff?' Aaron asked her. 'We found an old TV set over on Britton Island once.'

'Seriously?' Nessa said. 'How did a TV set end up on a beach?'

'Probably fell off the back of a boat, like all the other junk that ends up on our beaches,' Charlie said. 'Trust me, my dad's found way worse stuff than that when he's been out on patrol. At least a TV set's too big for a turtle or seabird to swallow. But plastic bags and containers aren't. He's even found toothbrushes and disposable razors. Imagine if you were a turtle hatchling trying to make your way out to sea through all that rubbish.'

Bindi nodded. Plastic was becoming a huge problem in oceans all over the world.

'I once found a mobile phone,' said Rocky. 'It was out of credit though,' he added, making everyone laugh.

'We might need a special category for stuff that can endanger wildlife,' Bindi agreed. 'The main thing is we want everything that's brought in to be recorded and weighed and then added up to get a grand total at the end of the day. Then we can hopefully use that information to send the message to boat-owners that they need to be more careful about securing their stuff properly.'

Bindi checked her list again. 'Charlie? Your dad reckons you're pretty good at maths. I'd like to put you in charge of collecting all the figures from each weighing station, if that's okay with you.'

Charlie looked uncomfortable. 'Umm . . . could someone else do that, please? Rocky, maybe? It's just that . . . I've kind of already organised my own station for today.'

Nessa pretended to look shocked. 'Without running it past us first?' she joked. She turned to Bindi. 'Everything has to go through us, doesn't it, B?'

'Not necessarily, this is a group effort after all,' said Bindi, distractedly. She had been trying to figure out what Charlie had been up to for the past few days. He'd definitely been acting strangely – riding his old bike into town or down to the beach, and coming back carrying odd-shaped parcels.

And yesterday a huge delivery van from the hardware store had turned up at Charlie's house while everyone was having lunch. But Charlie had squirreled away the package into his studio and had disappeared behind its locked door for the rest of the afternoon. Bindi had noticed the same delivery van return early this morning to taking something away. It was all very mysterious.

However, if the only way to find out what was going on was to let Charlie run an unauthorised station, it was fine by her. 'Go for it,' Bindi finally told him, grinning.

'Oh, okay,' Nessa said quickly, equally puzzled about what Charlie was planning. 'So, what's next?'

'That's about it, I think,' Bindi said, checking her list one more time. 'Wicked is scheduled to play at 4 pm, just after we announce the results of the weigh-in and the total amount of ghost nets collected. But you guys already know that. And all the shops or community organisations from town that are running food or market stalls have already been briefed on where to set up.'

'What about the reporter that's coming from the *Minyalwuy Gazette*?' Nessa pointed out. 'They're going to want to interview someone.'

'You should do it, Bindi,' Jonah said. 'After all, you've done most of the organising.'

Bindi smiled. 'Thanks, Jonah, but it's not my town. One of you guys should do it – even you, Jonah, seeing as it was your idea to add the marine debris collection. I'm quite happy to work behind the scenes. Believe me, I get to do enough PR stuff during the rest of the year.'

'How about you and I do it together, Jonah?' Nessa suggested. She quite liked the idea of having her picture in the local paper. Who knew? The story might get picked up by one of the national newspapers, and she'd be on her way to stardom. She might even end up with her own TV show, just like Bindi!

Jonah shrugged. 'Happy for you to do it all on your own, Ness.'

Nessa grinned. This was turning out to be one of the best days of her life! Not only was her band going to be playing in front of the whole town, she was going to get her photo in the paper. 'Yes!' she squealed, giving the air a little victory punch.

Bindi smiled at her new friends. 'Okay, everyone,' she said, checking her watch. 'Project Wicked is T minus five and counting. Let's do it!'

CHAPTER TWELVE

'BINDI?' NESSA SAID. 'I THINK someone's calling you.'

Bindi put down the sheet of paper where she was keeping tally of the number of ghost nets that had been collected so far, and peeked through the window of the caravan. She'd been run off her feet by a steady stream of queries from stallholders and station minders all day, and she just wanted a few minutes of peace so she could get on with some important paperwork. But this time it was only Charlie standing there, his hands in his pockets.

Bindi slid the window open. 'Hey, stranger. How's your mysterious stand going?'

Charlie grinned, then shrugged. 'Why don't you come and see for yourself?'

Bindi didn't need to be asked twice. Closing the window, she scuttled down the caravan's steps to join him. 'So where are we going, exactly?' she asked, barely able to contain her excitement.

'Be patient,' Charlie laughed. 'Why do you always have to know everything before it happens?'

Bindi shrugged. 'Just curious, I guess. Dad

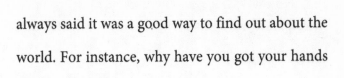

always said it was a good way to find out about the world. For instance, why have you got your hands in your pockets?'

'Because they're blue!' Charlie said, pulling them out and waggling them in her face.

'With splodges of green and silver,' Bindi said, taking a closer look. 'Is that paint I can smell on them?'

'Sure is,' Charlie said, stopping outside a marquee set up on the edge of the footy oval. 'Come in, I've got something for you.'

Intrigued, Bindi followed him into the marquee. Inside, groups of kids were sitting around trestle tables, busily painting and decorating square pieces of hardboard. Bowls of shells, seed pods, small pieces of dry coral and other natural materials had been placed at regular intervals along the tables, interspersed with shallow containers of paint and tubes of glue.

'Hi B!' Robert called, waggling his hand at her. He was sitting with Leila, one of Charlie's cousins, who was busy gluing a series of shells along the bottom edge of her square board.

Bindi waved back, grinning. So *this* was what Charlie had been doing for the past few days – setting up an art studio for the clean-up day! She should have guessed he'd do something like this, it was such an original idea.

Charlie handed her a piece of hardboard and a thick brush. 'This is your square,' he told her. 'You can decorate it however you like, but you must use at least two of the colours I've put out on the tables. And you *must* include the shape I've outlined on the board with pencil,' he added, pointing to a curving line on the right-hand side of her square.

'I'm not sure about all of these musts,' Bindi mused. 'What if I want to paint something else? Like an elephant?'

'You can if you want,' said Charlie, looking a little disappointed. 'But then you'll ruin my surprise.'

'Only joking,' Bindi laughed. 'There's no way I could paint something that looked even vaguely like an elephant! It would probably get mistaken for a duck or an umbrella or something.'

'That's a relief,' said Charlie. 'My project will only work if everyone follows the guidelines exactly as they're asked to.'

'You're definitely a man of mystery, Charlie,' laughed Bindi, picking up a brush and dipping it in some silvery blue paint. She began to spread the paint across the square, taking care to stay within the boundaries of her outlined shape.

'Let me know when you've finished,' Charlie said, moving across to another table to help a little girl with her brushstrokes. 'Maybe we could go for a walk or something? Check out some of the other stalls?'

'Sure, that sounds great,' replied Bindi. She could do with some fresh air after being cooped up in Nessa's family caravan all morning. And it would be great to have a chance to see how well all their plans had worked out. 'See you then.'

Charlie and Bindi strolled around the sports reserve, visiting the various weighing stations to see how much rubbish had been collected so far. Bindi was looking forward to finding out the grand total, and people were already hazarding guesses as to what the final amount might be.

'I reckon it'll reach at least a tonne, maybe more,' Aaron suggested. 'You should see how many bags of plastic have been emptied into the skips so far.'

'Anyone found any mobile phones yet?' Charlie asked.

'Two, actually,' Aaron replied, grinning. He turned to Rocky and gave him a playful shove. 'And guess what? Neither of them had any credit left on them either.'

'Ha ha,' said Rocky, rolling his eyes. 'You're never going to let me live my mistake about the mobile phones down, are you?'

He handed Bindi a litter pack. 'Here you go, B. We noticed you hiding in the caravan all morning. Now's your chance to get out and do some real work like the rest of us. Off you go, and don't come back until it's full!'

'Are you kidding me?' Bindi began, then stopped when she realised Rocky was pulling her leg. 'Actually, I'd quite like to do some rubbish collecting,' she announced, realising it would also be the last chance she'd have to see the area before her family flew out the next morning. 'Come on, Charlie, I'm sure your painting project can run itself for a while.'

'Yeah, okay,' he said. 'I think most people have got the idea of what to do now.' He pointed to a path that led from the reserve and down to the shore. 'Let's go that way. There's a creek along there where rubbish often collects after a storm or high tide.'

'Cool,' said Bindi. 'Sounds like the perfect place.'

CHAPTER THIRTEEN

THE TWO FRIENDS WOUND THEIR
way over a little bridge and down to where the
mouth of the creek met the ocean. Charlie's
suspicions had been correct – there was plenty of
litter to be collected.

Bindi set to work straightaway, bending down
to retrieve a bottle from a twisted mangrove root.

'Hey, it looks like someone had the same idea as us.' She pointed to a spot a bit further along the creek, where a blond boy and girl were having an argument.

'Ssshh,' said Charlie. Crouching down, he put his finger to his lips, reminding Bindi of the day she and Charlie had gone out to Crocodile Creek with Eddie.

Bindi hunkered down beside him. 'Why?' she whispered, puzzled.

Charlie looked at her as if it were obvious. 'I want to hear what they're saying.'

'Because . . .?'

'Because it could be funny,' said Charlie. 'People often say funny things when they think no one else can hear them.'

'Okay, but just for a minute,' said Bindi. 'I need to get back to see how the tallies are going.'

'Let Nessa worry about that for a while. I bet she's spent the whole morning preening in front of the mirror to make sure she looks good for the photographer this afternoon.' Charlie shot her a knowing grin. 'Am I right?'

Bindi nodded. 'Pretty much.' Not only was Charlie a good artist, Bindi realised he was also a great judge of character. Maybe the two things went together. You had to know your subject really well if you were going to capture its likeness on the page, even if it was an animal. *Especially* if it was an animal. That was something that had really stood out about Charlie's paintings. It was like he had captured the complete essence of each creature. Not many people had the ability to do that.

Bindi suddenly found herself missing her pets. Everyone knew that Bindi had lots of favourites amongst the wild animals at Australia Zoo. Like Savannah, the white rhino, for example, or the cheeky cheetah cubs, Josh and William. But not many people knew about Diamond, her German shepherd, or her horse, Harry.

The thing she missed most of all was taking Diamond to the beach for a swim. Though, with the constant danger of saltwater crocodiles, she'd have to be careful if she ever brought him to Minyalwuy.

A twig cracked, breaking her train of thought, and she realised that the boy and girl were heading their way.

'Maybe we'd better just stand up and get out of here,' Bindi whispered to Charlie. 'They might think we're spying on them.'

Charlie made a patting motion in the air with

his hand, indicating they should stay exactly where they were. 'Too late,' he hissed. 'If we move now, they'll spot us for sure.' He pointed to the thick curtain of leaves that surrounded them. 'Besides, they won't be able to see us in here – the vegetation's too thick.'

'I hope so,' said Bindi, feeling like she was an actor in a crime show. Now that the boy and girl had moved closer, she realised she knew who they were – Samantha and Ryan – the two kids she and Robert had spoken to about yellow crazy ants that first morning in the permit office. So much had happened since then, Bindi hadn't given the siblings a moment's thought since.

'Haven't you collected enough rubbish yet?' Ryan moaned to his sister. 'I want to get out of here already.'

Samantha waggled her bag at him. 'Just a few more pieces,' she told him. 'You want to win the prize for the most rubbish collected by an individual or duo, don't you?'

Bindi did a double take. 'We're awarding prizes?' she whispered to Charlie. 'I don't remember that bit. It's definitely not on my list of "Things to Do".'

'Maybe the mayor stepped in at the last moment to offer them,' Charlie suggested. 'He likes to get the council involved with things like this.'

'Hey, that's great –' Bindi began, forgetting to lower her voice.

'Ssshhh,' Charlie reminded her, putting his finger to his lips again.

There was a slapping sound, followed by another angry outburst from Ryan. 'That's it, I'm out of here!' he snapped. 'I've just been bitten by a sandfly for the gazillionth time. I'm still covered in itchy bites from the last time we went into the bush.'

'Fine!' his sister snapped back. 'Let's just go then. But don't blame me when we don't win the prize, after all the effort I've put in today.'

She was just about to storm off when she stopped stock still, staring at her brother in horror. He was sitting down on the muddy creek bank, pulling off his socks and shoes.

'Ryan, what are you doing?'

'Taking off my shoes so I can dip my ankles in the creek,' he told her. 'My bites are so itchy I can't stand them any longer. I need something cool on them to dull the pain. Besides, it's really hot up here, or hadn't you noticed?'

Bindi tapped Charlie's knee. 'Come on, let's

go. I don't feel comfortable listening in to people's private conversations like –'

Charlie suddenly grabbed Bindi's arm and gestured wildly for her to stop talking. Startled, she complied. 'Maybe his sister hasn't noticed the heat,' Charlie whispered. 'But something else could have noticed her brother. You don't sit with your feet dangling in the water in croc country.'

Bindi took a deep breath and slowly let it out again. 'I can't believe he'd be that silly!'

Charlie pointed to the surface of the creek. 'A croc could be watching them right now. See how there are weeds and reeds over there?'

Bindi nodded grimly. 'And the ripples in the water.'

'You'd never see a crocodile if it was stalking you,' muttered Charlie.

'We're going to have to warn him somehow,' Bindi whispered . . .'

'We're going to have to warn him somehow,' Bindi whispered, her mind racing. 'We need to get him to move away from the edge of the creek.' Bindi was reminded of seeing a croc snatch a wild boar off the riverbank at the Steve Irwin Wildlife Reserve. It had happened so quickly, the pig didn't even have a chance to squeal!

This time, however, there were people involved. People who should have known better. Bindi couldn't stand by and watch any longer. Without another word, she raced down to the bank to warn Ryan.

CHAPTER FOURTEEN

'AND THE WINNER OF THE prize for the most rubbish collected by an individual or duo goes to . . .'

Bindi stole a glance at Samantha and Ryan. Both of them, still white as a sheet from their experience by the creek, seemed dazed and completely oblivious to the proceedings. Bindi couldn't blame them. Even though everything had turned out okay in the end, Ryan's actions had been foolish and dangerous. She bet it was the last time he'd cool off his itchy bites in a creek again!

'. . . Old Mick and his faithful pal, Bella!'

The crowd erupted into a loud cheer. Everyone in town loved Bella, but they had a soft spot for Old Mick as well. It was great see him back on his feet and doing so well after losing everything he'd owned in the fire.

'And that concludes the individual and group awards for the day,' announced the mayor. 'Now, on to more important news. If I could just invite a couple of the members of the team responsible for today's wonderful event up to the podium . . .' He peered at the piece of paper he was holding. 'And they call themselves . . . let me see . . . Project . . . uh . . . Project –'

'Wicked!' screamed Nessa and Bindi, hugging each other in excitement. Things had gone way beyond any of their expectations, which had been pretty big to start with!

'Come on, Bindi,' Jonah said, pushing her towards the makeshift podium. 'Up you go. We couldn't have done any of this without you.'

Bindi shook her head. 'Nuh-uh,' she said, refusing to budge. 'Like I said, this is your town and these are your people; I'm just a visitor for the week. Nobody even knows who I am!'

'Well, *somebody* has to go,' Nessa said. 'The mayor's standing there waiting for us.'

She was right. The speeches couldn't move on

until someone from the organising team went up on stage.

'Rocky?' Bindi suggested.

Rocky took a step back. 'No way!'

'Aaron?'

'Forget it! I'm too shy!' he insisted. 'Send Charlie up instead. He always knows what to say.'

But Charlie seemed to have disappeared. In the end, Nessa grabbed Sam and Jimi, and dragged them up onstage with her. Cameras flashed as she shook the mayor's hand and took a deep bow.

Bindi grinned. If Nessa was serious about getting into a career in show business, she certainly had the right attitude for it!

'Give them a big hand, everybody!' the mayor announced. 'Three cheers for Project Wicked!'

Once the foot stamping and whistling had died

down, the mayor handed Nessa a piece of paper. 'And now, if I could just get you to read out the official tallies for us,' he announced, passing her the microphone.

'Ahem,' began Nessa, clearing her throat. 'The total amount of ghost nets cleared from beaches today is . . .' She looked out at the crowd. 'Where's the drum roll when you need it?' she asked cheekily, making everyone laugh.

'Okay, okay, I'll be serious now,' she continued. 'The total amount is . . . 36!'

'Wow,' said Jimi, reaching for the microphone. 'That's almost half the amount cleared away from around here in a whole year.'

'And that's at least thirty-six marine creatures' lives we've saved, because they now won't be caught up in nets,' Sam added proudly.

Nessa paused while the crowd clapped wildly, then resumed announcing the results. 'And finally, the total amount of marine debris collected across all weighing stations is . . .' This time, the crowd provided a mock drum roll for her by stamping their feet. '. . . 1.2 tonnes. That's a lot of rubbish, everyone, so well done!'

Bindi gazed up at the podium, her eyes shining. Project Wicked had done it! In the short space of only a few days, they'd actually achieved what they'd set out to do. A smile spread slowly across her face as she realised something else.

'Quick,' she said to the others, 'someone give me a pen and a piece of paper.'

Jonah handed her a biro and a serviette from the sausage sizzle. Bindi quickly scrawled a few words on the serviette, then handed it back to him.

'Could you take this up to Nessa and ask her to read it out? You'll have to be quick, though, before she leaves the podium.'

'Sure,' said Jonah, looking puzzled. He sprinted over to the official area and shoved the serviette into Nessa's hand, just as the mayor called upon everyone to give the team a final round of applause.

'What's this?' Nessa whispered, staring at the scrawl on the crumpled serviette.

Jonah shrugged. 'I've got no idea,' he whispered back. 'Bindi wants you to read it out.'

Nessa quickly scanned the words, and grinned. She now understood *exactly* why Bindi wanted her to read the message to the crowd.

Grabbing the microphone back from the mayor,

Nessa asked for quiet so she could make one last announcement. Then, in a clear, resonant voice, she said, 'See, everyone? Kids *can* make a difference.'

CHAPTER FIFTEEN

BINDI CLAPPED ALONG WITH the rest of the crowd to Wicked's first song, an original number Nessa had written for the band about achieving her dreams. She was certainly well on the way to doing just that, Bindi realised.

When the second song started, she slipped away from the others and headed for the marquee where

Charlie had set up his temporary art studio. She was eager to find out exactly what his plans were for all those coloured squares he'd had people decorating all day long. Hopefully, everything would now be revealed.

But Bindi arrived to find the marquee empty. Everything had been packed up and taken away. Puzzled, she headed back to the stage to look for Charlie. He never did anything without a good reason, and Bindi was determined to find out what that was before her family left town.

The first person she saw was her brother Robert, bopping along to the music with a couple of other kids.

'Hiya, B! Wicked are really wicked, huh?' he shouted, busting some crazy dance moves. 'Do you reckon they're going to record an album?

I reckon I know heaps of kids who would buy it back home.'

'Me too,' Bindi said, ruffling his hair. 'Have you seen Charlie anywhere?'

Robert shook his head. 'Nope, not since I did my painting in the marquee this afternoon. That was awesome fun.'

'Okay. Well, if you see him, will you let him know I'm looking for him?'

'Sure thing,' said Robert, turning back to his friends.

Bindi kept moving through the crowd, asking everyone she knew if they'd seen Charlie. No one had seen Eddie for a while either, it seemed. Bindi wondered if they were perhaps together somewhere.

She was just about to give up when she felt

something lick the palm of her hand. She whirled around.

'Bella!' Bindi cried, giving her a pat. 'Congratulations on helping to win the award!' Bella threw her head back and barked, then nuzzled in close for another pat.

Bindi rubbed Bella's ears in the place Diamond liked to be patted, then turned to her owner. 'Hey Mick, have you seen Charlie recently? Or Eddie? They both seem to have vanished.'

Old Mick grinned. 'Matter of fact, I have. I've just come back from the clubhouse. They wanted me to let them in. Said they had a present for the club or something and told me not to worry, they'd fixed it all up with the owner.'

'Don't suppose you could run me over there, could you?' she asked Old Mick. She wasn't sure why but she had a really strong feeling she needed to be there with them.

Old Mick sighed. 'Right you are. I was just coming back to have a cup of tea and a bit of a chinwag with some of me mates while I listened to the kids in the band, but I guess I get to hear them enough down at the club, eh?'

He gestured with his chin towards an old weather-beaten station wagon parked a few metres away. 'That's my car over there. Hop in and I'll run you over to the clubhouse. Hope you don't mind the smell of dog, though. Bella always insists on sitting in the front seat, and what Bella wants these days, Bella gets.'

'Not at all,' laughed Bindi. 'I wouldn't have it any other way.'

Within minutes, they'd arrived at the clubhouse.

Bindi was relieved to hear Eddie's familiar voice as she crossed the lawn. But she still couldn't figure out why he and Charlie were here. What could be important enough for them to leave the mayor's presentation? Charlie should have been up there on that stage with the others, soaking up all the congratulations.

She opened the door and stepped inside. Charlie and Eddie were busy packing up ladders and tools. She was just about to call out to them when something else in the room caught her eye.

On the wall facing the ocean was a mural made up of dozens of multi-coloured squares. There were blues and greens of every shade, silvers and greys – some with textured surfaces, others smooth. The shells and coral glowed softly in the evening light. The mural was beautiful – truly beautiful. But it was the way the pieces came together to form a whole that brought tears to her eyes.

At the heart of the mural was a snubfin dolphin, skimming joyously across the shimmering waves.

'Charlie,' she whispered, shaking her head. 'This is amazing. How did you –'

Charlie spun round. 'Oh, Bindi. Hi,' he said, his cheeks flushing. 'You weren't supposed to see this yet. It's not quite finished. I still have to –'

'Looks pretty finished to me,' Bindi said. She stepped forward, tracing her fingers over one of the panels. 'It's for the snubfin we found in the ghost net, isn't it?'

Charlie nodded. 'Yeah, I couldn't stop thinking about it. I thought there must be something I could do to help celebrate its life – something that would allow it to live on in people's memories.' He paused, trying to find the right words. 'And, well, this just seemed to be one way to do that.'

'And an exceptionally wonderful way to achieve that,' his father said proudly.

'But why didn't you tell everyone what you were doing?' Bindi wanted to know. 'Why all the mystery?'

Charlie shrugged. 'I didn't want to take attention away from Project Wicked or the band. This was *their* day.'

Eddie put away the last of the tools, and stretched. 'Talking of Project Wicked, do you think we can go back to the party now? I promised your mother a dance.' He grinned. 'I reckon Bindi could do with a bit of time out as well, after all the work she's put in over the last few days. What do you say, guys?'

Bindi grinned. She intended to spend her last

night in Minyalwuy having as much fun as possible. 'Definitely.'

'Right then,' Eddie said. 'We better see if we can get Old Mick to take us back again, before everyone goes home!'

There were plenty of sleepy faces the next morning as Eddie dropped the Irwin family off at the airport for their flight home.

'I understand how remote this place is,' Terri yawned, 'meaning there's only one flight out per day. But why does it have to be *so* early in the morning?'

After the celebrations had finally wound down the night before, the members of Project Wicked and their families had all gone out for well-earned pizza. Afterwards, they'd gathered at the clubhouse to admire Charlie's tribute to the snubfin dolphin. Realising how successful the day had been, they'd made a decision to make Project Wicked an annual event. Except next time, Nessa had suggested, they'd invite a TV crew up to film everything, rather than just a reporter from the local paper!

A voice came over the loudspeaker, announcing their flight was ready for boarding. Bindi collected her boarding pass from her carry-on bag, then turned to Eddie and Marlena.

'Thanks for having me,' she said, giving them each a hug. 'I've had an absolutely fabulous time here.' She turned to Charlie. 'And you have to promise to keep working on your art, okay? No matter where you're living.'

'You bet,' he grinned, handing her a small flat

parcel wrapped in tissue paper. 'Ummm . . . this is just a little something to remind you of your stay in Minyalwuy,' he added shyly.

'Hey, thanks, Charlie,' said Bindi, touched by the gesture. She peeled back the layers of tissue to reveal what was inside – a tiny, perfect painting of a snubfin dolphin, just like the one from the mural.

'It's beautiful,' she whispered, giving Charlie a hug.

Terri squeezed her shoulder. 'Come on, B, it's time to board.'

'Coming,' Bindi said. She carefully placed the painting inside her carry-on bag, then joined the queue at the boarding gate, her mind fizzing with memories of the last few days.

The last thing she saw as she headed towards

the plane was a large white banner arching across the tarmac.

'*Nhäma yilala*,' the words on the banner read. And underneath, the translation: 'See you later'.

Bindi intended to do just that.

SNUBFIN DOLPHINS (ORCAELLA HEINSOHNII)

The snubfin dolphin was only recognised as a new species of dolphin in 2005. They have a short, stubby dorsal fin and a round melon-shaped head. Unlike most other dolphin species in Australia, they don't have a beak and their mobile neck has a distinct crease around it. Snubfins vary in colour from pale white to brownish grey, and reach an average length of around two metres. They are shy animals that like to socialise and interact in close-knit family groups of six to fifteen.

Appearances of snubfin dolphins have been recorded around the north coast of Australia, arching from Western Australia to Queensland, where they inhabit rivers, estuaries and coastal waters.

The World Wildlife Fund is currently helping to develop a rescue plan for the species as it is estimated that less than 1,000 snubfin dolphins exist in the wild. This is a result of the combination of their low reproductive rate, and external threats such as commercial fishing and the pollution, degradation and destruction of their habitat.

Wildlife Warriors work to save snubfin dolphins and other marine animals by removing ghost nets and other rubbish from North Queensland beaches and waterways. To find out more about the protection of Australian wildlife, please visit:

www.wildlifewarriors.org.au

★★★★★

COLLECT ALL SIX BOOKS IN THE BINDI BEHIND THE SCENES SERIES!

★★★★★

bindi

BEHIND THE SCENES

The Wildlife Games

bindi

BEHIND THE SCENES

An Island Escape

bindi

BEHIND THE SCENES

Bouncing off the menu